A Yearly Academic Planner for the "A" Student

Copyright 2016

All Rights reserved. No part of this book may be reproduced or used in any way or formor by any means whether electronic or mechanical, this means that you cannot recordor photocopy any material ideas or tips that are provided in this book.

Month :

time	Monday -	√

Assignments

To do List :

time	Tuesday -	√

Assignments

time	Wednesday -	√

Month:

time	Thursday -	√

Assignments

time	Friday -	√

time	Saturday -	√

Assignments

time	Sunday -	√

Notes

To do List :

Upcoming Tests

Month :

time	Monday -	✓

Assignments

time	Tuesday -	✓

To do List :

time	Wednesday -	✓

Assignments

Month:

time	Thursday -	√

Assignments

time	Friday -	√

time	Saturday -	√

Assignments

time	Sunday -	√

Notes

To do List :

Upcoming Tests

Month:

time	Monday -	✓

Assignments

time	Tuesday -	✓

To do List:

Assignments

time	Wednesday -	✓

Month:

time	Thursday -	✓

time	Saturday -	✓

Assignments

Assignments

time	Friday -	✓

time	Sunday -	✓

Notes

To do List :

Upcoming Tests

Month :

time	Monday -	✓

Assignments

To do List :

time	Tuesday -	✓

Assignments

time	Wednesday -	✓

Month:

time	Thursday -	✓

Assignments

time	Friday -	✓

time	Saturday -	✓

Assignments

time	Sunday -	✓

Notes

To do List :

Upcoming Tests

Month :

time	Monday -	✓

To do List :

time	Wednesday -	✓

Assignments

time	Tuesday -	✓

Assignments

Month:

time	Thursday -	✓

Assignments

time	Friday -	✓

time	Saturday -	✓

Assignments

time	Sunday -	✓

Notes

To do List :

Upcoming Tests

Month :

time	Monday -	√

Assignments

To do List :

time	Tuesday -	√

Assignments

time	Wednesday -	√

Month:

time	Thursday -	√

time	Saturday -	√

Assignments

Assignments

time	Friday -	√

time	Sunday -	√

Notes

To do List :

Upcoming Tests

Month:

time	Monday -	✓

Assignments

time	Tuesday -	✓

To do List:

Assignments

time	Wednesday -	✓

Month :

time	Thursday -	✓

Assignments

time	Friday -	✓

time	Saturday -	✓

Assignments

time	Sunday -	✓

Notes

To do List :

Upcoming Tests

Month :

time	Monday -	✓

To do List :

time	Wednesday -	✓

Assignments

time	Tuesday -	✓

Assignments

Month:

time	Thursday -	✓

time	Saturday -	✓

Assignments

Assignments

time	Friday -	✓

time	Sunday -	✓

Notes

To do List :

Upcoming Tests

Month :

time	Monday -	√

To do List :

time	Wednesday -	√

Assignments

time	Tuesday -	√

Assignments

Month:

time	Thursday -	√

time	Saturday -	√

Assignments

Assignments

time	Friday -	√

time	Sunday -	√

Notes

To do List :

Upcoming Tests

Month :

time	Monday -	√

Assignments

To do List :

time	Tuesday -	√

Assignments

time	Wednesday -	√

Month:

time	Thursday -	√

Assignments

time	Friday -	√

time	Saturday -	√

Assignments

time	Sunday -	√

Notes

To do List :

Upcoming Tests

Month:

time	Monday -	✓

Assignments

To do List:

time	Tuesday -	✓

time	Wednesday -	✓

Assignments

Month :

time	Thursday -	✓

Assignments

time	Friday -	✓

time	Saturday -	✓

Assignments

time	Sunday -	✓

Notes

To do List :

Upcoming Tests

Month :

time	Monday -	✓

Assignments

To do List :

time	Tuesday -	✓

time	Wednesday -	✓

Assignments

Month:

time	Thursday -	✓

Assignments

time	Friday -	✓

time	Saturday -	✓

Assignments

time	Sunday -	✓

Notes

To do List :

Upcoming Tests

Month :

time	Monday -	√

Assignments

To do List :

time	Tuesday -	√

Assignments

time	Wednesday -	√

Month:

time	Thursday -	✓

time	Saturday -	✓

Assignments

Assignments

time	Friday -	✓

time	Sunday -	✓

Notes

To do List :

Upcoming Tests

Month :

time	Monday -	√

Assignments

time	Tuesday -	√

To do List :

time	Wednesday -	√

Assignments

Month :

time	Thursday -	√

time	Saturday -	√

Assignments

Assignments

time	Friday -	√

time	Sunday -	√

Notes

To do List :

Upcoming Tests

Month:

time	Monday -	✓

Assignments

To do List:

time	Tuesday -	✓

Assignments

time	Wednesday -	✓

Month :

time	Thursday -	√

Assignments

time	Friday -	√

time	Saturday -	√

Assignments

time	Sunday -	√

Notes

To do List :

Upcoming Tests

Month :

time	Monday -	√

Assignments

To do List :

time	Tuesday -	√

Assignments

time	Wednesday -	√

Month:

time	Thursday -	√

time	Saturday -	√

Assignments

Assignments

time	Friday -	√

time	Sunday -	√

Notes

To do List :

Upcoming Tests

Month :

time	Monday -	√

To do List :

time	Wednesday -	√

Assignments

time	Tuesday -	√

Assignments

Month:

time	Thursday -	√

Assignments

time	Friday -	√

time	Saturday -	√

Assignments

time	Sunday -	√

Notes

To do List :

Upcoming Tests

Month:

time	Monday -	√

To do List:

time	Wednesday -	√

Assignments

time	Tuesday -	√

Assignments

Month:

time	Thursday -	✓

time	Saturday -	✓

Assignments

Assignments

time	Friday -	✓

time	Sunday -	✓

Notes

To do List :

Upcoming Tests

Month:

time	Monday -	✓

Assignments

To do List:

time	Tuesday -	✓

Assignments

time	Wednesday -	✓

Month:

time	Thursday -	√

Assignments

time	Friday -	√

time	Saturday -	√

Assignments

time	Sunday -	√

Notes

To do List :

Upcoming Tests

Month :

time	Monday -	✓

To do List :

Assignments

time	Tuesday -	✓

time	Wednesday -	✓

Assignments

Month:

time	Thursday -	✓

Assignments

time	Friday -	✓

time	Saturday -	✓

Assignments

time	Sunday -	✓

Notes

To do List :

Upcoming Tests

Month :

time	Monday -	✓

Assignments

To do List :

time	Tuesday -	✓

time	Wednesday -	✓

Assignments

Month :

time	Thursday -	√

time	Saturday -	√

Assignments

Assignments

time	Friday -	√

time	Sunday -	√

Notes

To do List :

Upcoming Tests

Month :

time	Monday -	✓

Assignments

time	Tuesday -	✓

To do List :

time	Wednesday -	✓

Assignments

Month:

time	Thursday -	√

Assignments

time	Friday -	√

time	Saturday -	√

Assignments

time	Sunday -	√

Notes

To do List :

Upcoming Tests

Month :

time	Monday -	✓

Assignments

To do List :

time	Tuesday -	✓

Assignments

time	Wednesday -	✓

Month :

time	Thursday -	✓

time	Saturday -	✓

Assignments

Assignments

time	Friday -	✓

time	Sunday -	✓

Notes

To do List :

Upcoming Tests

Month :

time	Monday -	✓

Assignments

To do List :

time	Tuesday -	✓

Assignments

time	Wednesday -	✓

Month:

time	Thursday -	√

Assignments

time	Friday -	√

time	Saturday -	√

Assignments

time	Sunday -	√

Notes

To do List :

Upcoming Tests

Month :

time	Monday -	√

Assignments

To do List :

time	Tuesday -	√

Assignments

time	Wednesday -	√

Month:

time	Thursday -	√

Assignments

time	Friday -	√

time	Saturday -	√

Assignments

time	Sunday -	√

Notes

To do List :

Upcoming Tests

Month :

time	Monday -	√

Assignments

To do List :

time	Tuesday -	√

Assignments

time	Wednesday -	√

Month:

time	Thursday -	✓

Assignments

time	Friday -	✓

time	Saturday -	✓

Assignments

time	Sunday -	✓

Notes

To do List :

Upcoming Tests

Month :

time	Monday -	✓

To do List :

Assignments

time	Tuesday -	✓

time	Wednesday -	✓

Assignments

Month:

time	Thursday -	√

Assignments

time	Friday -	√

time	Saturday -	√

Assignments

time	Sunday -	√

Notes

To do List :

Upcoming Tests

Month :

time	Monday -	✓

To do List :

time	Wednesday -	✓

Assignments

time	Tuesday -	✓

Assignments

Month:

time	Thursday -	✓

Assignments

time	Friday -	✓

time	Saturday -	✓

Assignments

time	Sunday -	✓

Notes

To do List :

Upcoming Tests

Month :

time	Monday -	√

To do List :

time	Wednesday -	√

Assignments

time	Tuesday -	√

Assignments

Month:

time	Thursday -	√

time	Saturday -	√

Assignments

Assignments

time	Friday -	√

time	Sunday -	√

Notes

To do List :

Upcoming Tests

Month :

time	Monday -	√

Assignments

To do List :

time	Tuesday -	√

time	Wednesday -	√

Assignments

Month:

time	Thursday -	✓

Assignments

time	Friday -	✓

time	Saturday -	✓

Assignments

time	Sunday -	✓

Notes

To do List :

Upcoming Tests

Month:

time	Monday -	✓

Assignments

To do List:

time	Tuesday -	✓

Assignments

time	Wednesday -	✓

Month:

time	Thursday -	✓

time	Saturday -	✓

Assignments

Assignments

time	Friday -	✓

time	Sunday -	✓

Notes

To do List :

Upcoming Tests

Month :

time	Monday -	√

Assignments

To do List :

time	Tuesday -	√

Assignments

time	Wednesday -	√

Month:

time	Thursday -	√

time	Saturday -	√

Assignments

Assignments

time	Friday -	√

time	Sunday -	√

Notes

To do List :

Upcoming Tests

Month :

time	Monday -	√

To do List :

time	Wednesday -	√

Assignments

time	Tuesday -	√

Assignments

Month:

time	Thursday -	✓

Assignments

time	Friday -	✓

time	Saturday -	✓

Assignments

time	Sunday -	✓

Notes

To do List :

Upcoming Tests

Month :

time	Monday -	✓

Assignments

To do List :

time	Tuesday -	✓

time	Wednesday -	✓

Assignments

Month :

time	Thursday -	✓

time	Saturday -	✓

Assignments

Assignments

time	Friday -	✓

time	Sunday -	✓

Notes

To do List :

Upcoming Tests

Notes

To do List :

Upcoming Tests

Notes

To do List :

Upcoming Tests

www.ingramcontent.com/pod-product-compliance
Lightning Source LLC
LaVergne TN
LVHW080456160826
845677LV00006B/1381

* 9 7 9 8 8 6 9 4 4 4 7 9 0 *